BASKETBALL YOGA

BASKETBALL YOGA

BALL IS LIFE

TONY WISE

ILLUSTRATED BY
SHILOH GREEN

Tony Wise
Basketball Yoga

All rights reserved
Copyright © 2024 by Tony Wise

No part of this publication may be reproduced, distributed, or
transmitted in any form or by any means, including photocopying,
recording, or other electronic or mechanical methods, without the prior
written permission of the publisher, except in the case of brief quotations
embodied in critical reviews and certain other noncommercial uses
permitted by copyright law.

Published by Spines
ISBN 979-8-89383-304-1

CONTENTS

1. INTRODUCTION

Basketball yoga! When you hear the term yoga, you automatically start thinking of postures and breathing techniques. Now, basketball yoga, what postures are we doing with a basketball? You might say, no postures here. Basketball yoga is the paradoxical union between life and ball. Just as in the game of basketball, there are so many similarities in the game of life. Allow me to share my perspective with you on basketball yoga. To ball is to live! It's all one and the same. The word yoga in Sanskrit means union. We will take a phenomenal journey to understand how the union between the game of basketball can help you win in the game of life. To be one with the ball is to be one with life.

As you look at this picture above, you see an image of absolute balance. Now ask yourself one thing, is balance an illusion?

Basketball yoga allows you, the reader, to come up with your own viewpoint by sharing a new philosophy of basketball and life. "BYOGA!" The way of the ball.

2. PREPARATION

In the game of life, it serves you well to be prepared. In basketball, preparation is absolute. If you desire to win, there's only one answer: "Practice." I say practice, work on your dribbling drills, work on your shooting drills, work on your rebounds, work on your layups, work on your endurance. I say work, work and work some more. Basketball is a game that flows and ebbs; its perpetual motion is quite similar to the ocean. The one constant is that the ball never gets tired. As in life, no matter what you do or don't do, the one constant is that time keeps moving. I've played ball for well over 40 years. What I've experienced and observed is that you can spend hours in the gym, days in the weight room, and months on the treadmill, but if you do not strengthen your mental fortitude all will be in vain. The mental strength it takes to push beyond your human limitations is essential in the game of life and in basketball. That is what separates greatness from average. When nothing seems to work and you're missing every shot, the energy it takes you to push through and not fall into despair is like a supernova from the sun. Life comes at you, whether you are prepared or not. You study your hardest for that final exam and come up short. It appears that every obstacle is in your way. You give all to your job, give all to your family and fall short of their expectations. It will take a great amount of energy to keep your joy.

Mental fortitude definitively is the game changer. Take for example, Kobe Bryant, one of the greatest players ever to play the game of basketball. Kobe's season never stops. The guy is borderline psychopathic, obsessive. He works on his game constantly. How can Kobe, one of the greats, improve himself? He attacks the game relentlessly, never complacent, never complaining, and never satisfied with his ability. Kobe was consistent with his method. He loves the game and it drives him.

Imagine approaching life with that vibrato, to love life, to tune in, to know you and to seek joy in all the faucets of life. Ask yourself this question. Am I living the best version of my life? Are you joyful? For those who play the game of basketball, have you ever played a tight game, battling, and giving all to the game? Nothing else matters but what happens between the lines. The world stops, time merely vanishes. That you can say is joy, especially when you win the game, and you are elated. Theodore Roosevelt states, "It is not the critic who counts; not the man who points out how the strong man stumbles, or where the doer of deeds could have done them better. The credit belongs to the man who is actually in the arena, whose face is marred by dust and sweat and blood; who strives valiantly; who errs, who comes short again and again, because there is no effort without error and shortcoming; but who does actually strive to do the deeds; who knows great enthusiasms, the great devotions; who spends himself in a worthy cause; who at the best knows in the end the triumph of high achievement, and who at the worst, if he fails, at least fails while daring greatly, so that his place shall never be with those cold and timid souls who neither know victory nor defeat." This sums up the game of basketball. Those few lines reflect living life. Prepare to live joyously, what can be more ecstatic?

3. FOUR QUARTERS

Basketball is a game that has four quarters. The key to winning is winning every quarter. It doesn't matter how you start the quarters; it's truly about winning every quarter. Winning in life is similar, it doesn't matter how you start, every person is unique, but their quarters are the same. Life starts with you as a baby, an adolescent, a teenager, an adult. We all die, we all have challenges. Does that make sense to you? We all die. We were born to die. Imagine this. You are up 15 points in the first quarter of a game, and then you start coasting, and stop playing defense. What do you think will happen? My guess is, the chances of winning that quarter just dropped dramatically. It works the same way in life, no matter what stage of life you are at. As soon as you think you know it all and begin to coast, the game changes and funny twists and turns begin. We have no idea why this happens. My only suggestion is to take every quarter as your last. Play as if your life depended on it. Live to the fullest, live your best life, and do all that you can do. Leave it all on the court.

When the quarter is done, you know you did all that you could have possible have done. The first quarter is the toughest one; it really sets the tone for the rest of the game. Life is the same actual setup. You need to prepare in the early stages of your life, and this will influence the later stages.

You put in the work; you do what others won't do today in order to get your results for tomorrow. When everyone decides to coast, you go hard trying to win the quarter.

In the game of basketball, there's an old saying. "Every

shot you don't take, you are guaranteed to miss". In the game of life there is an old adage that says, "Those who are prepared to win usually do". There is a funny thing about each quarter you play. They all start off slow, however somewhere between the tip off and the whistle blowing, the game speeds up and poof the final buzzer rings. If that's not hilarious think about your life. One day you are running around in diapers, and the next thing you know, you are 40 years old with 3 kids. Life is funny. If you sit back and analyze the whole thing in its entirety, all you can do is laugh. Why are we born to die? First quarter, second quarter, third quarter, fourth quarter, then game over. In the blink of an eye, the score board goes off. Cherish every moment of the game, stay off the bench as much as you can, play lights out. Take every shot that you can and go hard. No matter what the fans say about you when you are on the court, the one thing you know they will all agree upon is that you played every quarter as though it was your last. You left it all out on the court, lights out. One of the challenges that every ball player faces, and it's the biggest challenge in life, is staying the course.

4. FOCUS

In today's society, everyone is being programmed to multi-task; it has become the greatest thing since sliced bread. Let's examine our physical makeup. All of our sensory organs are pointed out. We collect so much data in one day. Our eyes see a million variables a second, our ears hear everything, our nose is constantly bombarded by scents, our skin feels everything, and all of this data is being recorded. The body operates at the speed of light, gathering data, however we only use what we need. Think about how many things occur in our bodies simultaneously. The heart pumps blood, we are breathing, and the kidneys filter toxins. The bladder excretes toxins and the pancreas regulates our glucose levels. Each body part knows its function and performs just that one task. It focuses on doing just the job assigned to it. Now, here we go determined to do five and seven things at the same time consciously. In the miracle, that is our body, each organ, each system only does one thing, total focus. Our brains are unique. We have the reticular activating system that blocks out the data we collect, and only makes us aware of what we need to use. We have our reptilian brain that warns us of danger, either fight or flight. We have the subconscious, conscious and mind. The subconscious operates all our body functions, giving us autonomy to do other things.

You wonder why it's so difficult for us to stay focused. There are too many moving parts, however in this jambalaya it works.

In the game of basketball, we have many moving parts, the center, the point guard, the shooting guard, the small forward and the power forward. Each member of the team has a specific function, however in order to have a championship team each individual must connect and operate as a unit, the body. One focus, one mission, one aim. Life in all its intricacies plays on the same stage. In life we give ourselves so much to do; we find a million activities to worry about, even trying to manage stress. Why would you spend your time managing stress which is clearly no good for you? We spend our lives majoring in minor things. We are multi-taskers, sounds good. If using your life energy to do multiple assignments at once works for you, then it's a good thing for you, however how do you feel? Are you joyful? We must defend our right to choose to live rather than purely exist.

5. DEFENSE

Sun Tzu, one of the greatest military strategists of all time says, "invincibility lies in the defense; the possibility of victory in the attack". Invincibility lies in the defense. Really contemplate this line. In the game of basketball, there are many defensive strategies. To name a few, we have man to man, box and one, two 1 two, two 3, trapping, pressure coverage, and zone coverage. In all these different strategies, the common element remains the same. Do not let the other team score; prevent them from scoring at all costs. If they can't score, they won't win. Sounds easy, doesn't it?

In life, defense is a must because you are constantly being attacked. Why is it that in today's society humanity, health and your mind are not sacred grounds? It's all-out warfare. People have chosen to be discriminative, my way or no way. Do you watch the news? Are you listening to the music of this generation? Are we defending humanity? Think long and hard about this. Life is what you make of it. Life begins with you, and it's all within you. Do we really know life? Do we truly understand the miracle of what this life contains? Protect it at all costs, protect your humanity, protect your health, and protect your mind. We are not perfect, however we are unique beings. For those who know the name Peter Parker, do you recall what he was told? "With great power comes great responsibility". We are blessed with the greatest power ever, life. Yet so many of us are irresponsible about it. Take charge and defend your life at all costs. Defend your basket. However, for you to win the game, you must attack. Without a shadow of a doubt, you have to score buckets.

6. OFFENSE

Buckets swish like only nets. There is no sweeter sound to a ball player than the swish of the ball buckets. If you have ever had the pleasure of playing the game of basketball, then you know this feeling. Scoring is an intricate part of the game. One of the most rewarding feelings ever is when you make a basket. It looks simple when you are on the sidelines, but trust me it's far more technical than it looks. There are several factors in shooting. The height of the rim is ten feet, and the rim diameter is about 18 inches. The ball has a circumference of 29.5 to 30 inches and weighs 18 to 20 ounces. Gravity is constantly working against you and the earth is always spinning. Everyone holds the ball a little differently; however finger positioning is instrumental in scoring buckets. Did I mention that gravity is always working against you? Anyone can make a basket; however, the consistency of making baskets after baskets, that's proficiency. That's what separates the great ones. Life rewards those who are consistent and makes legends out of those who are proficient.

You always have to be offensive minded in life and you have to attack. The reason for this is that success is relative to each individual and their values. True success is achieving a goal that you have set for yourself. That's all success is. Legendary status is gained by developing mastery over proficiency. When others say it's impossible, you show them possibility. That's the nature of having an offensive mindset in life. You never quit, you never stop, and you keep pushing and hammering away. To be a juggernaut, you have to be relentless. There is no short cut to legendary, however you do need to adjust your offense from time to time. There are no one-set formulas. The game is constantly evolving. Adapt or die. Make buckets and win.

7. ADJUSTMENTS

In every great recipe there lies a secret ingredient. In basketball there is only one. Coach John Wooden explains it like this: "Adaptability is being able to adjust to any situation at any given time". Basketball is a game of streaks, momentum and strategy, however adjustments are paramount. Great coaches know when a defensive strategy is no longer effective. What might work defensively in the first five minutes can easily work against you in the next seven minutes of a quarter. A great offensive player knows when he must adjust his game. If the jumpers aren't falling, you've got to start driving to the hoops. If driving to the hoops isn't working, you've got to become a facilitator. You are constantly reevaluating the game, and the game within the game. Life is no different. Think about it, what you do to overcome one situation in the morning might not work to overcome the same situation at night. Life in its purest form is fluid, but it does not travel in a straight line.

There is no one set plan for all. Remember, life is funny. Think about the planets and our solar system. Do you know that the planets do not move in a perfect orbit? The planets are bobbling all over the place. What keeps them from smashing into one another is truly miraculous. Another thing is, there's always daylight somewhere on the planet. So, our creator in his or her infinite wisdom purposely adds changes and variety to our existence. We have four seasons on the planet, and we have four quarters in our lives. We have constant changes every day. No two days are alike. First, we start young, and then we get old. Didn't we say this life is so funny? You are always adapting, always adjusting, and you have to reevaluate the game inside the game. This is the secret to the game. We have to execute our strategies, we have to adjust to each play, and most importantly, we have to play our position on the team. No one person can win a game by himself. He can make the winning shot, but someone has to pass him the ball. That's the nature of it all.

8. TEAMWORK

There are no I's in team, however there is me. What that simply means is that you must hold yourself accountable. You are accountable for the task given on defense. Guard your man. You are accountable for executing the play on offense. You are accountable to your team, to bring it, perform with intensity, and stay focused on the game 1000% of the time. There will always be an exceptional player on a team, because he transforms his desire into will. That's the only difference, his commitment to the game is on a high level and anyone can get there but few push through to reach there. We've seen great players score 50 points in a game and lose. That's good for personal stats, but the objective of the game is to win. No one player can win a game by himself. Basketball wasn't designed that way. It takes total team commitment; that's why we have five players on the court.

Our creator, in his or her infinite wisdom, gave us life with the same formula. You are not created old; you start out as a baby, who is dependent on his or her parents, team. You usually have an extended family, grandparents, cousins, uncles, aunts and other siblings. There is an old African proverb that says, it takes a village to raise a child, a team. No one achieves greatness by themselves. There is always something or someone that sets a spark, lights a fire that helps the great one to realize greatness and if you should ever ask a player like Stephen Curry, Kevin Durant, Larry Bird, Magic Johnson, LeBron James, Michael Jordan, Bill Russell or Kobe Bryant, where did it start? They will all have some variation of the same story. It might have been a parent, or an early coach, or someone they admired who lit the fuse, however they did the work. They worked, no excuses, constantly practicing, until it all clicked, perfect mastery of their desired craft. That's life. Finding your passion early, getting mentored, and putting in the work is the formula that will lead you to a joyful and blissful existence. After all, that's truly the ultimate exercise in living, to be joyful and blissful in all that you do. Win the game!

9. GAME TIME

This is where the ball meets the court. All the hours of preparation, both physically and mentally, all the late-night practices running drills after drills, and pushing your body past your pain threshold. Yes, do you feel that energy? For you ball players, close your eyes and think about that feeling you get when you strap up your laces, take that deep breath, and walk on the court. It's bliss! Here is the funny part of life. After all you did to prepare, you might go zero for ten shooting, shoot a couple air balls, misjudgment on your passes, and blow defensive assignments. Welcome to game time. That's just the facts of the game. Sometimes the craziest things happen on the court, for example miss timing a rebound the ball hits your finger full speed then whack, broken finger. What do you do then? Kobe snapped his back into place and finished the game. That's the true definition of beast mode however when it happened to me, I left the game went to the hospital they snapped it back into place, I thought about my whole life, I wondered why now, I was killing them on the court that day, it took me eight months before I strapped up and played a game. The mind is a powerful machine and whatever you tell yourself sure believe it intensifies it by ten. I made it out, started slowly, paced myself and played. Life happens to us all, however here is the secret sauce, make your adjustments. For most of us, all we need is a little time on the bench to settle down, while others need to take a deep breath and play through it.

If you've played this game long enough, sooner than later you're going to find that sweet spot. Some call it being in the zone, some call it joy. There comes a point in the game when the basket becomes extremely big, when every decision you make is on point, and your ability to read the defense is lightning speed. Every shot you take is a bucket. Life is like that. When you are able to impose your will on the game of life, and become aware, the game opens up for you. There is no magic to it. You have to dominate, be relentless. You determine the outcome of your life, plain and simple. How you approach your life's journey is 100% up to you. Your preparation is totally up to you. Your ability to handle each adversity, every challenge and all obstacles will determine the game. Life is truly up to you. You can make it joyful or you can make it miserable. So take full joy in the process, play the game with true reverence, respect the game and score buckets.

10. BASKETBALL YOGA WORKOUT

Here are some simple exercises or asanas in which you can practice basketball yoga. Before you start anything, stretch. Get on your toes and touch the sky. Stretch your spine, stretch your limbs, stand erect, left leg cross in front of right and touch the ground, then do the reverse. Stretch your arms, stretch your fingers, loosen your wrist, and stretch your neck. The key here is to have your body free, no tension. Before you touch the ball, visualize yourself on the court at the free throw line taking practice shots. When doing so, the key here is to breathe. Take a full breath, inhale, then hold on for 3 seconds, then exhale. You can start by doing figure eights. You stand almost in a sitting position, feet spread apart to shoulder width, then you place the ball between your legs from front to back, then switch hands. Come around drawing the number eight. Put the ball back through your legs, from left side to right or vice versa. You can start off by doing 20; the key is to do as many as you can in 5-minute intervals, resting for 2 minutes, then continuing for 30 minutes. You can also do standing scissors, a simple process of putting the ball between your legs while you are jumping front and back one leg at a time, making a scissors cutting motion. Breathing is essential. The key here is to breathe out on the left leg, and inhale on the right keeping in sequence with your motion. The key here is to do as many as you can in 5-minute intervals, resting for 2 minutes and then continuing for 30 minutes.

Drink water in between each 30-minute interval, however, just drink enough. Do not over consume it. Breathing properly and just enough water intake will do wonders. Finally, you can do what I call "run the lines". The court consists of a series of lines. You have the baseline, the free throw line, and the half line. All you have to do is run from the baseline to the to the free throw line, then go back to the baseline. Go from the baseline to the half court line then back to the baseline. Go from the baseline to the other side of the court's free throw line, then back to the baseline. From the baseline to the other side of the court's baseline and back to the baseline. The key here is to do as much as you can in 5 minutes, rest for 2 minutes and then continue for 30-minute intervals. Completion of these three simple basketball exercises will have you looking and feeling like the champion you are. If you do these simple workouts three days a week, eat properly, and drink lots of water, you will feel the changes.

www.ingramcontent.com/pod-product-compliance
Lightning Source LLC
Chambersburg PA
CBHW040957110726

48007CB00004B/36